Divine Economy
And Its Real World
Economic Principles

Divine Economy
And Its Real World
Economic Principles

Bruce Koerber

iUniverse, Inc.
New York Lincoln Shanghai

Divine Economy And Its Real World Economic Principles

iUniverse books may be ordered through booksellers or by contacting:

iUniverse
2021 Pine Lake Road, Suite 100
Lincoln, NE 68512
www.iuniverse.com
1-800-Authors (1-800-288-4677)

ISBN-13: 978-0-595-35083-4 (pbk)
ISBN-13: 978-0-595-79784-4 (ebk)
ISBN-10: 0-595-35083-6 (pbk)
ISBN-10: 0-595-79784-9 (ebk)

Printed in the United States of America

Dedicated to Dr. Roger Garrison,
who introduced me to classical liberalism
and to my wife Jeanne
and my two daughters, Natalie and Leah.

"There cannot be too much of a correct theory."
Ludwig von Mises

Contents

List of Illustrations

1

Introduction

What would it take to bring together the theory and the reality of the economy? How can the current and past plight of humanity be reconciled with the human potential for good? New insight into the economy will come shortly, as it is presented in this book; and that insight will reveal new possibilities.

The origin of the economy is intricately bound with the origin of man which all of you know is ancient and even still a mystery. It taxes all the discerning powers of historians and archeologists to discover the origin of man. Why does this veiled past have anything to do with the economy? The premise of this book is that the economy is a uniquely human institution and that without the human being there would be no such thing as the economy. Speaking in these terms it sounds obvious that they appear and evolve concurrently.

The intimately woven fabric of humanity and of the economy necessitates a deep examination into the nature of mankind. The human urge to act is irresistible. Human action stems from the same source as human reason. Although rudimentary in the early stages of development, the early actions taken by primitive human beings were of the moment and yet they were also agents of transformation. There is a dynamic here, spontaneity between the act and the transformation; a dynamic that conveys great meaning. One does not exist without the other and yet each spark of interplay reveals new possibilities. It is the cumulative effect of human actions taken throughout time that brings to us the modern economy.

A moment of reflection is needed to be able to discern what is real and foundational. As I just mentioned, the economy is a uniquely human institution. The potential then exists for the economy to be in one of two states, since the human being can dwell in the world of perfection or imperfection. If the higher nature of humanity is realized then the institution that is a tool for the expression of human action will, itself, be elevated and celestial. It is the divine nature of the human being which is his true reality and therefore it can be deduced that the highest potential of the institution of the economy is divine.

1

What is the current condition of the modern economy? It is true that the modern economy carries the cumulative effect of human actions taken over time; consequently along the way unnecessary burdens have been added. These add weight and bulk. And the burdens are cumulative. The metaphorical divine charger cannot traverse the span of contemporary history nimbly and ably. It may stumble. It may have to reverse or change courses. These burdens slow the arrival of the triumph of prosperity, which is our birthright provided we recognize our divine nature.

We must sort out the reason for the burdening or weakening of the institution that serves to bring about our betterment. Understanding human nature sheds some light on the subject. The will to choose the higher perfections versus choosing the imperfections of our lower nature is at the crux. Ego-driven intervention is an example of the exercising of our lower nature. Just as metal oxidizes and becomes corrupt, so too the economy deteriorates when it is corrupted by intervention.

Herein lays the beginnings of the problem that needs to be dealt with using economic science. The economy as a human institution has not been seen, up until as is now proposed, as divine. How do we know what the uncorrupt economy looks like if it is never seen as having a pure form? Even those who recognize that the economy operates perfectly well, independently (as implied in "laissez-faire"), have not made the connection to the divine nature of the human being as an essential identity. This is a new thought and is worthy of consideration. Granting that the economy is divine implies the following: that the actors are seen as expressive agents of the will of mankind; that there is no omniscience within the realm of human policy-making that can even minutely compare to the divine expression inherent in the market; and that the market is not a product of human design.

The market is a divine institution that emerges spontaneously from human action. It is a social institution that forms for the sake of production. The market is the time and place where the convergence of all of this useful information transpires and is discovered. Every exchange takes place in a market, which makes clear the point that the word 'market' is most certainly universal and almost infinitely broad. As stated with eloquence by Mises:

> Choosing determines all human decisions. In making his choice man chooses not only between various material things and services. All human values are offered for option. All ends and all means, both material and ideal issues, the sublime and the base, the noble and the ignoble, are ranged in a single row and subjected to a decision which picks out one thing and sets aside another.

Nothing that men aim at or want to avoid remains outside of this arrange-
ment into a unique scale of gradation and preference. The modern theory of
value widens the scientific horizon and enlarges the field of economic studies.
[1]

It is clear then that subjective values are in the realm of economics. When an
exchange does occur it is based on the knowledge-at-hand by the actors, the
buyer and the seller. The knowledge-at-hand is relative and imperfect yet, at the
same time, it is fully coordinated within time and space. It could not be made
more perfect as evidenced by the willingness of both the buyer and the seller to
consummate the exchange, free of any coercion to do so.

There are those who object to the imperfect knowledge of the actors, insisting
that they would have made a better decision if they had perfect knowledge. This
objection is certainly naïve and contrary to the real world. Human beings are neither omniscient nor omnipresent. They cannot grasp all that came before nor do
they know the future with certainty. All actors in the economy have only partial
knowledge. The "single mind" that has all knowledge does find expression in this
new concept of a divine economy through the divine institution bestowed upon
mankind, that is, the unique human institution that forms the foundation of economics—the market. Human planners of the economy are hopeless failures and
can be more aptly described as oppressors. In the real economy, the divine economy, there is a 'central planner' who is all-knowing and all-seeing and perfectly
just. It is God. God is the creator of the economy as a human institution and His
design allows the fullest expression of human diversity. In the divine economy
there is decentralized planning to the nth degree, where n represents each individual or business entity that is actively interacting within the market process. The
economy changes as the human race changes and yields its promised fruits condi-
tionally—depending upon whether the current state of affairs exists as either a
hampered or an unhampered market.

The state of affairs at any point in time reflects the spiritual maturity of mankind and its corresponding condition of the economy. As mankind as a whole
matures, he increasingly cares for himself and for others. The economy always
fully serves at the level it is capable of as a human institution. Like all institutions
it has the appearance of structure. Its structure in its pure form is the market, free
from political intervention. The closer the economy is to a free market the greater
its capacity to be a full expression of a divine economy.

Remember that there is interplay between the human actors and the market
itself. There is a commingling of these two divine entities and both benefit from
this process of discovery. There is a transforming power in this divine encounter.

This is perhaps the most essential element of the divine economy. There is a divine power, the power to transform the resources bestowed upon us into goods and services and which then enables us to serve one another as a tribute to our loving Creator. The divine economy has the power to awaken us to our own potential which finds expression in service to one another and to our loving Creator. That is why the progress of humanity, even for us as individuals, depends on a free market. Likewise, the discovery of the merits of the divine economy depends on the educative process—significantly derived from the market experience itself—from which proceeds the ever-advancing progress of humanity.

Finally there is a critical need to bring all of these processes of the divine economy into the realm of science. Here the groundwork has already been laid by the great minds who have described the methodology of subjectivism and more specifically praxeology, which is the study and logic of human action. This great scientific heritage pays tribute to monumental thinkers such as Carl Menger, Ludwig von Mises, Fredrick von Hayek, Murray Rothbard and George Reisman. From their work and the work that continues along these lines there is a scientific foundation that provides the tools needed to test and to advance the understanding of the processes at work.

Since human beings act purposefully the power to make the divine economy manifest rests with each individual. It rests; it resides, and becomes evident in these actions. Mises writes:

> As long as a man lives, he cannot help obeying the cardinal impulse, the *elan vital*. It is man's innate nature that he seeks to preserve and to strengthen his life, that he is discontented and aims at removing uneasiness, that he is in search of what may be called happiness. [2]

The power to make the divine economy manifest comes from the invisible world of thought and reason and enters the visible world through purposeful action. No action occurs in a vacuum; therefore each action becomes a part of the educative matrix of actions, all of which follow the same subjective processes.

What is incredible is how the subjectivist methodology of classical liberalism allows the merging of science and religion. This subjectivist methodology can be used to discern the essential laws that apply universally to human beings when they are at the threshold of action, whether that act is an act of faith or a material act. These universal laws ultimately underlie our quest to know and understand. We are educated and make advancements by these insights. In the realm of faith our souls progress and our nature becomes more divine. In the material realm we become aware of how our interconnectedness can bring prosperity and how we benefit personally from that prosperity. This parallels a statement attributed to the British mathematician and metaphysician Alfred Whitehead, as quoted by Hayek, "Civilization advances by extending the number of important operations which we can perform without thinking about them."[3] The divine economy is inseparable from human civilization, nor is it separable from the advancement of human culture, at the individual or social level. The divine economy operates in accordance with the Will of God and it is a vehicle for the expression of the will of man. The implication of the divine economy is that there are laws and that there is order. The power within and without is beyond our grasp. Yet throughout history men have sought to grasp it. For the short while that they clutched the economy it corrupted them, and the economy became distorted and diverted, leading to the suffering of many, both near and distant. Ultimately the destiny of mankind was slowed by their intervention. Quoting Rothbard:

> "The hidden order, harmony and efficiency of the voluntary free market, the hidden disorder, conflict and gross inefficiency of coercion and intervention—these are the great truths that economic science, through deductive analysis of self-evident axioms, reveals to us." [4]

There is only One Being omniscient enough to see all that happens in the market matrix and only One Being that is not wholly dumbfounded by what human minds see as uncertainty. The economy is divine, it is God's. The economy provides channels through which the grace and bounty of God flow. The economy, itself a divine institution, acts upon man since it is inextricably a part of the human operating system. The sooner we learn this and trust this the sooner we can learn how to use this institution to bring about peace and justice. The divine economy is here for our benefit. It forces us, acting man, to refine ourselves internally (heart and soul, spirit and intellect) and externally (human and non-human resources).

2

Divine Economy Model ©

Shortly I will begin to present a graphical representation of the divine economy model. As the model is presented; its interconnectedness, reciprocity and symmetry will be discussed. One analogy that may prove useful is that of a complex organism made up of components that are more or less differentiated. Ourselves, we are made up of systems and organs and tissues and cells. Likewise the divine economy model has universal laws, foundational elements, concepts and principles.

The center of the model is its reality and essence, summed up using the words 'divine economy.' These two powerful words clearly state the vital perspective of this model. These two words efficiently convey the source and the dominion. The implication here is far more magnificent than laissez-faire which merely suggests: not to meddle. It implies that the economy is above and beyond our human understanding and that it can be corrupted—corrupted by human intervention alone. And the dominion reaches everyone in their daily affairs; it is both pervasive and subtle. It is basic and connected to the necessary acts of every man and woman and by its conveyance of information it allows people to function.

Just as there are four cardinal directions; a north and south and east and west, the divine economy model has four petals. Gleaned from the knowledge and insight of many great thinkers I chose the following petals for the model: human spirit, transformation, law, and order. So what we have is the model in its simplest form:

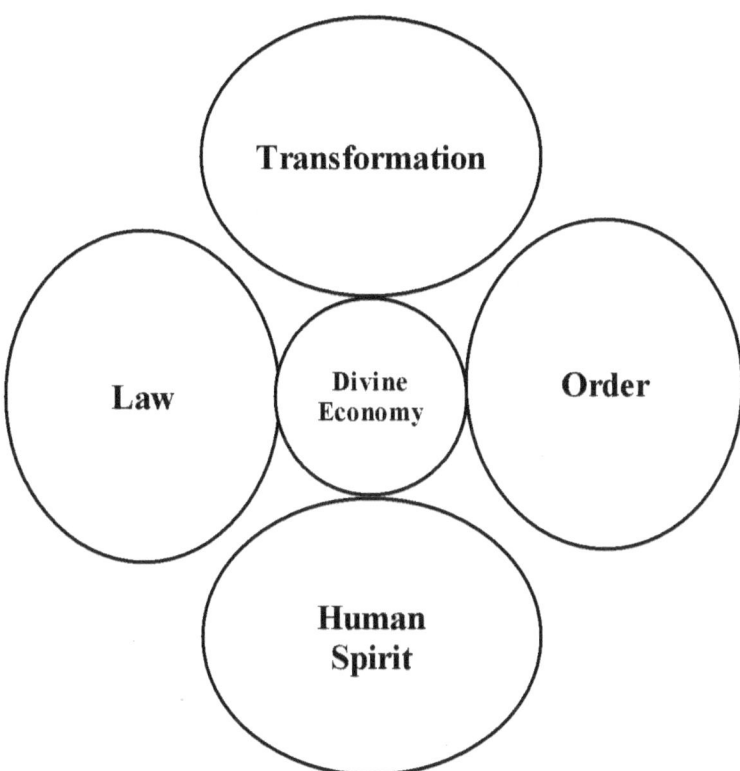

Diagram A–Anatomy of the Divine Economy

To the model we then add reciprocity and symmetry. The element of reciprocity adds the dimension of mutual exchange. Proportionality and relativity manifest themselves in the world and are expressions of the element of symmetry. The model now becomes:

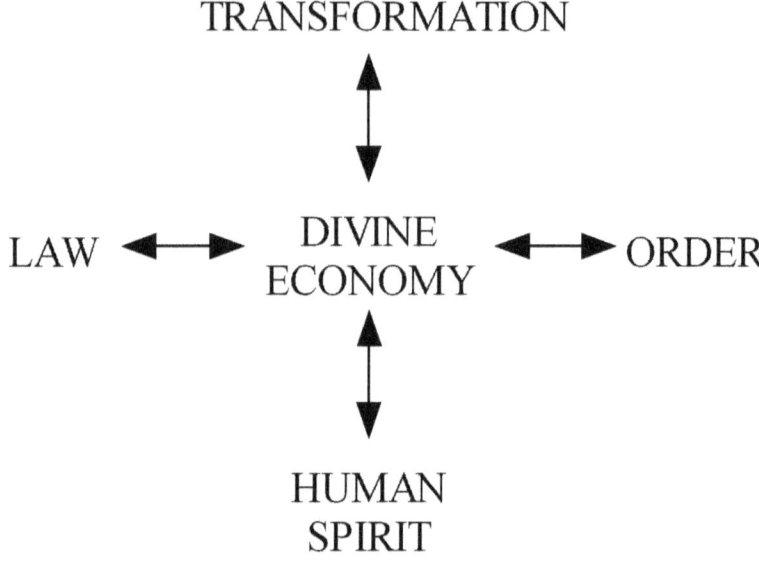

Diagram B–Skeletal Structure of the Divine Economy

In this form the functionality of the model begins to emerge. It has a dynamic nature. Every point is relative to every other point and every understanding gained causes movement—advancing civilization.

To continue to improve the functionality of the model more scientific elements of the economy are added. These economic elements were discovered by great thinkers in the tradition of classical liberalism. These certain points of focus are added to the four petals as intermediary potencies.

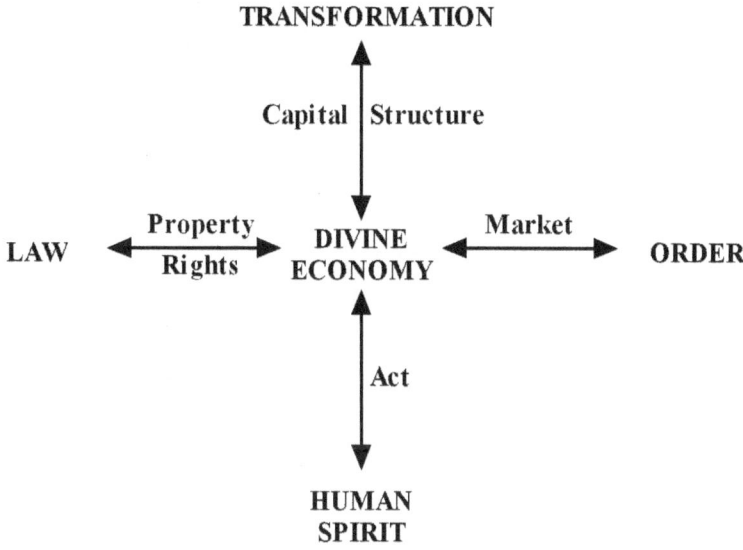

Diagram C–Modus Operandi of the Divine Economy

This is where the model begins to become complex. We will have to take a step back and examine more deeply the foundational components. Then the extremely potent intermediary elements will need to be explored.

Going back to the skeletal structure of the divine economy in Diagram B it is easy to see how interactive and cumulatively interactive it is. The human being has a nature that is subject to illumination. It is the human spirit that reflects that reality. Transformation is the illumination that takes place and this all comes about because we encounter the human spirit of others, directly or indi-rectly—there is no vacuum here. The world has structure and incorporating structure into our lives creates order. Transformation is furthered by discovering the operational laws of that order. The dynamic interaction of all of these interre-lated elements is certain. Already it is clear that the complexity of the divine econ-omy is mind boggling. We have to trust in the divine and content ourselves with understanding bits and pieces, ever humbled by the infinite greatness of the divine economy.

Moving on to the more complex model in Diagram C—the modus operandi of the divine economy—we need to spend some time educating and re-educating ourselves about these intermediary elements. It would be inaccurate and naïve to pretend that there is a common understanding of these four elements in the eco-nomic literature or in the minds of most readers. The four scientific elements that make up the modus operandi of the divine economy are property rights, human action, the market, and capital structure. These are potent forces which universally permeate human life on this planet!

Placement of these intermediate elements into the model relative to the initial foundational components expands the foundation of the model. The model readily accommodates the fluid manner in which these eight elements all juxtapose themselves.

Property rights interface closely with human action, the market and the capital structure. Property rights are truly foundational and have a strong connection to law in the divine economy since they anchor the economy to the human being. In its most basic and primary expression, property rights are human rights. The existence of a human being grants dominion, and its peaceful expansion toward food, clothing and higher attainments all fall within the domain of property rights.

The human spirit, each one a unique expression of the grace of God, becomes foundational in the divine economy through human action. Human action is the expression of the human spirit which implies that the human spirit is the locus of communication, and a channel for the two-way flow of knowledge. Understanding that the economy is a uniquely human institution means there is also cognition that the human spirit is where it all begins and human action is where it becomes manifest. Without human beings, whose nature it is to act purposefully, there would be no economy.

There is a saying: 'It takes two to tango!' That is what the market is. It is the place where the solitary individual becomes a social being. By this very broad definition the interaction of parents with their children could be considered a market. Although an argument could be forwarded against this line of reasoning such an argument serves no purpose here. The purpose of this broad definition is to remove the limiting definitions ascribed to the market and to remove the prejudices about the market. The market is where human action undergoes reconfiguration into a social entity. This is part of the dynamics between the 'act' and the 'transformation.' The market is where knowledge flows to and from in a civilization. And it is from this proverbial fountain of knowledge that order emerges.

Acting  Knowing

The three scientific elements just described—property rights, human action, and the market—are inherent and found in full potential in the divine economy. The fourth element differs slightly because of its very strong ties to time. Capital structure is also foundational. It contains and conveys the knowledge that all things in this world are subject to the law of time. Capital, the means of stretching production beyond the present, is foundational also. Most significantly, of all of the factors in the economy, capital is the most limiting. See if you understand why. Ponder—in the here and now, in the present, we cannot live in the future! That is our limitation. The reason capital is the most limiting is because it is what connects the present and the future in the economy. It is constrained by uncertainty yet its variation or structure determines the transformation that takes place in the economy. Since capital is the most limiting factor, the movement or advancement of civilization depends heavily upon the structure of capital. This necessitates, optimally, that the capital structure needs to be a harmonious expression of the market so that it truthfully reflects the will of the people. In the divine economy fully vested human beings find and share knowledge in the market. Part of that knowledge reflects the importance of time which becomes manifest in capital and its relevant structure.

The next modification of the divine economy model stretches the imagination a little by adding a depth dimension. This can be grasped fairly easily by imagining the modus operandi of the divine economy given in Diagram C as submerged in a bowl of water. The water that surrounds and supports the model represents latent and active entrepreneurship.

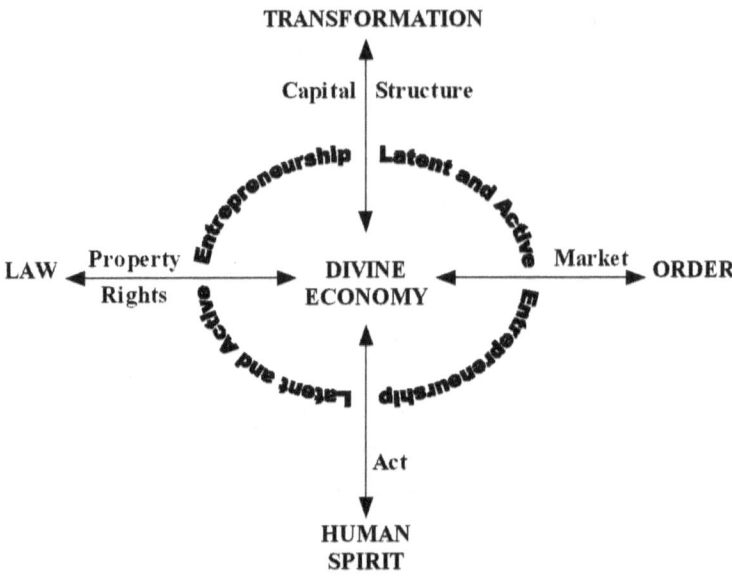

Diagram D–The Driving Force of the Divine Economy

Entrepreneurship is alertness to one's surroundings and the knowledge therein. When entrepreneurship is in the latent state the divine economy and its components are in potential only. When alertness triggers a response the result is active entrepreneurship, which significantly, is the driving force in the economy.

If I am in a latent state of entrepreneurship I may simply buy a product that I like. Or I may begin to actively perceive opportunities and compare and contrast to see what other products are out there to buy or sell. I may look at the time horizon, weigh the various possibilities, and decide to save so that I can buy a tractor. As an active entrepreneur I may discover discrepancies in the market that lead to inefficiencies and I may take steps to remedy the situation. When in a latent state, the water holds within it the divine economy. But when there is active entrepreneurship, energy is released which charges all of the elements in the water.

The final construct of the divine economy model is the identification of its poles. The divine economy has many components just like the complex system of the planet Earth which has numerous components such as the water cycle, the ocean currents, the atmospheric forces, geothermal forces, and absorption of solar radiation to name a few. The Earth also can be understood more fully by examining these factors as they are influenced by rotation around its poles. Similarly the divine economy can be more fully understood when the model includes the poles of unity and justice.

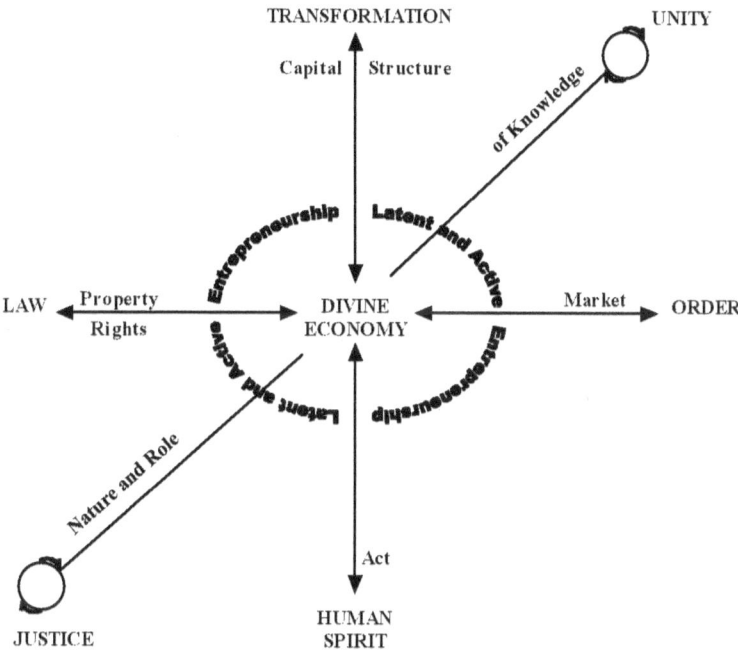

Diagram E—The Complete Divine Economy Model

It is around these two poles that the divine economy revolves. The axis of these poles represents the 'nature and role of knowledge.' The implication of this axis being centrally located within the model is: that knowledge flows throughout, and that free-flowing knowledge serves all of the divine economy processes best. Elaborating on the pole of justice—with justice the interest of the individual and those of society are inextricably linked. Justice also implies non-violence and non-coercion. Elaborating on the pole of unity—the pole of unity shines with prosperity for all—since there is now an awareness of the historical and scientific knowledge that shows all of humanity as one people. Bartolome de Albornoz wrote in the year 1573 A.D.:

> "Buying and selling is the nerve of human life that sustains the universe. By means of buying and selling the world is united, joining distant lands and nations, people of different languages, laws and ways of life."[5]

Now that the model is defined we are ready to connect it to the real world principles in the economic literature.

3

Real World Economic Principles

With the foundation of the conceptual divine economy model laid out it now becomes possible to insert economic principles into the model, fully aware of their interconnectedness. The locus of placement in the model is arbitrary yet logical. The logic of placement can be deemed a mental exercise, forcing one to examine the interconnectedness of economic principles. I take the liberty to begin the process.

To begin I divide the model into quadrants with two fundamental elements, one on either side of the quadrant. Dividing the model into quadrants then sets the stage for examination of economic principles that have a strong tendency toward:

A. human spirit/order
B. order/transformation
C. transformation/law
D. law/human spirit.

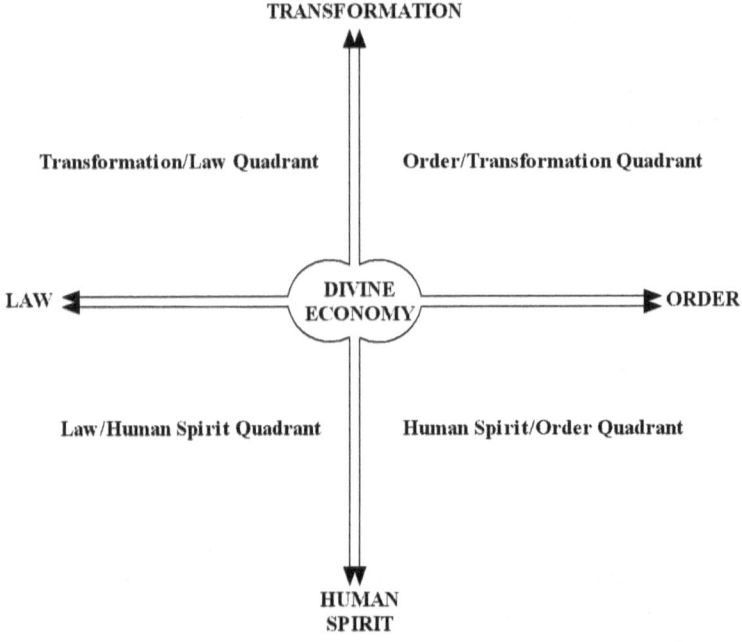

REAL WORLD ECONOMIC PRINCIPLES IN THE HUMAN SPIRIT/ORDER QUADRANT

I have chosen eight economic principles for placement in this quadrant. These are principles that exist in, emerge from, and complement both the human spirit and the social order. They find origin from human action and yet inspire human action. They find expression and are amplified in the market and at the same time continuously emanate knowledge by way of the market.

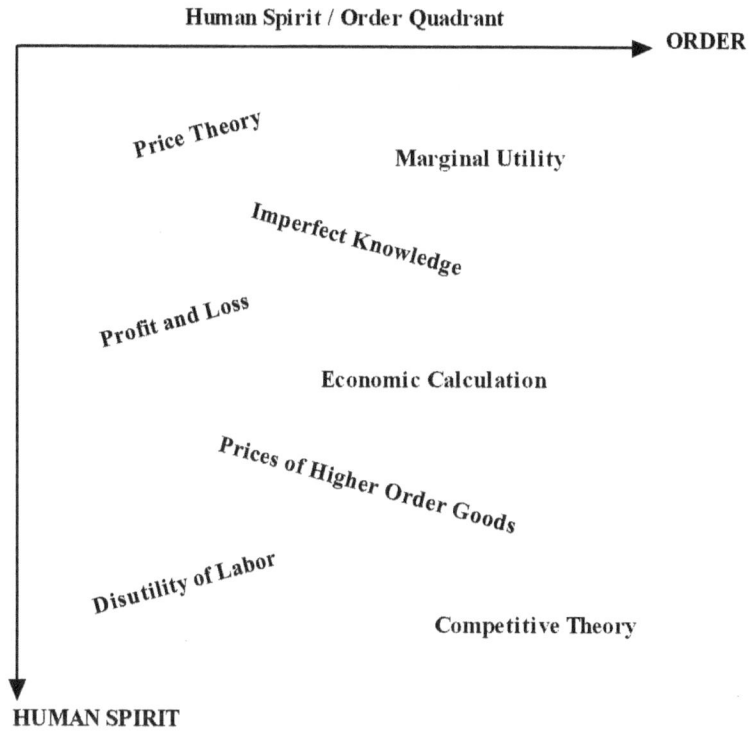

Economic Principles in the Human Spirit / Order Quadrant

Economic Principles in the Human Spirit / Order Quadrant

Price Theory

A good starting point is the law of supply and demand. If the supply of a good or service increases then the price decreases. If the demand for a good or service decreases then the price decreases.

The price of a good or service in the real world is relative to other goods and services and relative to the earlier price of that good or service itself. In other words, all prices are relative prices at the time and place of human action in the market. It is exactly that fact, that prices are relative to all others, that enables the price system to play an economizing role in decision-making. Let us assume that you go to a marketplace with $100, needing food and clothing and medicine but you find the market in a dysfunctional state—there are no relative prices. Only one price, the price of $45 for the clothing is known at the time. Would you know how to prioritize or whether to buy the clothing or not?

Quickly there is a need to define the market to offset commonly held prejudices against the market. The market is universal. It is a process where knowledge flows freely. The market is benevolent, profoundly cooperative, and quietly consultative in nature. The market is a conveyor of information just as is language. The following analogy is useful. Individually, I can speak to myself alone, or I can more fully use language and speak with others. The full benefits of language as a human endowment come from its social nature. If I happen to speak vulgarly, language as a human institution should not be attacked as being harmful. In fact, the social nature of language empowers it to have a moderating and refining influence on individuals, thereby lessening the occurrence of vulgarity. The market, likewise, releases the full benefits of the human spirit and all of the associated resources. If someone acts in a crude or frivolous manner it is not the fault of the market. In fact it is the social nature of the market that will tend to moderate and refine individuals, ultimately facilitating the advancement of civilization.

The price system finds expression in the market in the form of relative prices which conveys important information. For instance, factors which exhibit characteristics such as mobility or convertibility have a higher value than similar immobile or inconvertible factors. Another example, nominal wage rates mean little but real wage rates convey important information about the wage rate since it is then relative to other prices. Even if all prices are decreasing but the wage rate is decreasing to a lesser degree then the real wage rate is actually increasing. The market is the vehicle for conveyance of this valuable information and people make decisions or choices based on it.

Individuals in the market assess costs and revenues and continually modify their plans due to the signals that come as a result of changes in demand and supply. These adjustments demonstrate that the price system is both dynamic and efficient.

Marginal Utility

Closely allied to relative prices is the concept of marginal utility. The market conveys information about the plethora of relative prices of goods and services but ultimately active decision making by each person resides at the margin. The choice made is ultimately based on the subjective valuation about the perceived gain from the various choices. Whichever choice is perceived to bring the greatest satisfaction at the margin is chosen. Let us assume that I am very hungry and that I can buy either a pencil or an apple for a quarter. I will readily recognize the greater marginal utility of the apple and buy it.

Imperfect Knowledge

An insurmountable and an inescapable reality! As imperfect knowledge is moderated by having some knowledge and having some certainty people make decisions and act. Part of the uncertainty comes from the time element—the future. Another part of the uncertainty comes from a lack of information, and the corollary to this is the uncertainty about the other human beings on the planet and their decisions and actions. The relatively free and immediate flow of knowledge that is the potential of the market ameliorates this condition. The only certainties are: that there are uncertainties, that the world is dynamic, and that the market works best when it is unhampered.

Profit and Loss

Concomitantly there is no certainty that any effort made by a producer interacting in the market will yield a profit. It is a fact that any exchange that takes place during the market process occurs because of a double inequality of values. Will an exchange take place? Exchange occurs only when both parties value what they receive higher than what they give.

Involvement as an entrepreneur has risk because of uncertainty. The nature of the active entrepreneur is to be alert to opportunities; needs not being met or not be met as well as they could be. In the market it is possible that my perception as an entrepreneur is right or maybe it is wrong. It is possible that my perception that the resources that are needed may combine to serve the consumer wants better; or perhaps not. This is a constant ebb and flow that necessarily results from the uncertainty in the real world. The market encompasses all of the various facets, such as: profit and loss, entrepreneurship, communication, and knowledge; and the market conveys information in terms of relative prices.

In its earliest appearance in the primitive economy profit or loss was simply the outcome. If I raided a bird's nest I either found food or not. If my effort was not productive my failed effort represented my loss. If my effort was productive the food profited me. The profit motive is a necessary and inherent feature of the human operating system. As man and the economy evolved profits enabled producers to provide wages and other factor incomes for endeavors with lengthier production times.

Economic Calculation

Implied in the word 'calculation' is a basis of knowledge. It is from a basis of knowledge that the next step, that of calculation, can proceed. Implied in the word 'economic' is information about the economy, which is then disseminated via the market. But first things first! Private property happens to be an even more vital part of the market than the actual diffusion of knowledge, since all values spring from ownership and values are necessary for calculation.

The economy is dynamic and composed of trillions of needs and decisions that often change complexion. The basis of knowledge needed for economic calculation comes from the market in the form of relative prices. These prices are relative to all other prices at the current moment. The freer the market is, the quicker the information can flow and the greater the ability to correct errors. Desires, needs, and resources converge in the market and find full expression in the form of relative prices. Economic calculation involves comparing and contrasting and speculating about the relative prices expressed through the market.

Any attempt to calculate economically using fictional non-market values, values arbitrarily assigned by someone removed from the market, ignores the dynamic nature of the knowledge in the market which is tantamount to denying the human spirit. That is why vertical production in an excessively large firm results in bureaucracy and calculation error and that is also why socialism fails since it is an 'error-based institution.' What is mean by 'error-based' is the fact that the prices used for decision-making are arbitrary and imagined, not derived from the market process. These prices are erroneous and all decisions based on them are error-based.

Prices of Higher Order Goods

Not only does the market enable economic calculation but it extends beyond the here and now. The information in the market, the relative prices, also takes into account time. Goods which will reach the market in the future have a present value. And since they have value all the resources needed in their production have value. In other words, factor prices, too, are relative prices. However, without private property in factors of production there can be no factor prices, and without factor prices, cost accounting is impossible. To repeat, private property ownership is vital to the market. The economic calculation needed to realize profits, which pay the wages and factor incomes, depend on it. As decisions are made in the market between consumer goods and higher order goods, a bridge forms between the present and the future. This bridging of the present and the future leads to economic development.

Disutility of Labor

Exchange in the marketplace/market-process only happens if both parties feel that there is a gain. When an individual wishes to sell his services in the market he checks to see what the relative prices (wages for example) are and then must decide if the income is worth more than the alternatives, including leisure. However, if leisure is subsidized in any way then less of the labor factor becomes available, which reduces the productive capacity of the economy and sends waves throughout the economy like ripples emanating from a pebble dropped in a pond. If leisure is subsidized then relative prices throughout the economy will change, leading to aberrant decisions. There is nothing wrong with disutility of labor determining whether there is an exchange in the market as long as it is a true expression rather than one distorted by subsidy.

There is nothing wrong with the disutility of labor; in fact, the disutility of labor is actually a motive force. It inspires alertness to choices and alternatives. Subsequently, disutility of labor underlies entrepreneurship and it also underlies capital.

Competitive Theory

The natural tendency for humans is to make progress. That is what is implied in the act of exchange since it only takes place when both parties perceive a gain. This searching and questing and striving is part of the human operating system. That is not to say that there is not a disorder in the economy, like the example about the disorder resulting from subsidizing leisure. Making decisions at the margin, based on the relativities, and comparing where you are with where you want to be is natural and it is a human quality. Striving for excellence and refining oneself are meritorious expressions of this human trait. The knowledge that flows from the market-process provides the individual with 'data' in the form of relativities. Judgment about what is available, what possibilities exist, and about one's current condition, hinge on information available in the market.

Competition in the market is not a negative like it is in the animal world where 'survival of the fittest' is the outcome. The economy is divinely at the service of mankind. Competition in the market leads to new and better goods and services and means of production. With this advancing prosperity there are no long-run losers. Currently, corruption of the divine economy by ego-driven manipulators directs wealth towards favored ones and away from others, and this human intervention into the divine economy is what causes 'the rich to get richer and the poor to get poorer.' In contrast to the hampered economy, the net efficiencies that come from competition in a free market end up benefiting everyone.

Human Spirit/Order Quadrant Example

At a basic level each human being can distinguish between the ease or difficulty of the life task ahead. If a person is given a choice, that person will always prefer the easier of the two means of attaining their ends—as long as the task is not a personal recreational challenge or a personal development goal. What appears to be a non-productive urge, choosing the easy way, is actually a positive force. Disutility of labor is a sign of intelligence. It is a motivating force that leads to innovation. It inevitably causes advancement and progress.

Disutility of labor, despite its being an underlying law of purposeful action, has been corrupted and turned into a negative element in the economy under the current system of intervention. Why work when your basic needs are met if you don't work? Why provide excellent service when you get paid the same either way, plus you cannot lose your job? These interventions pervert the inherent power of this law that is part of purposeful human action.

Summary of the Human Spirit/Order Quadrant

The market is a time and place where information about relative prices is discovered. It is also a process within which knowledge flows. The market can be described as unplanned order. Not all knowledge is expressed as a price, but all knowledge is relative, and it is the market where knowledge is accessible to humans. It is economic action in the market that creates wealth. For the sake of human enlightenment and for the sake of human prosperity the market needs to be unhampered. Human intervention in the market is inevitably a corruption and a disruption of the divine economy.

REAL WORLD ECONOMIC PRINCIPLES IN THE ORDER/TRANSFORMATION QUADRANT

I have chosen nine economic principles for placement in this quadrant. These are the principles that find expression in and emerge from both the market and its capital structure. It is through the instrumentality of capital that the order of the market undergoes transformation. Equally symmetric and reciprocal is the vital need for the dynamic flow of information from the market-process so that capital can exist and its structure serve everyone's needs.

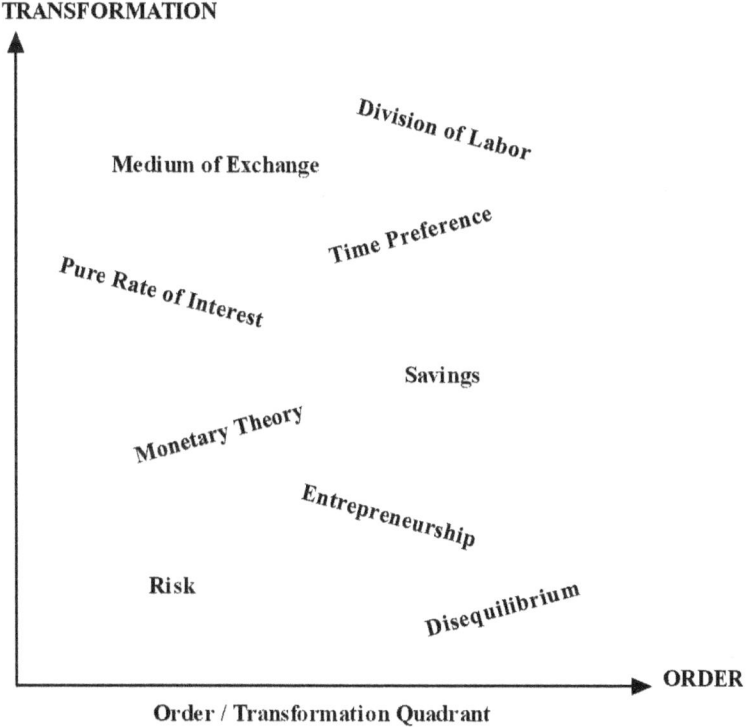

Economic Principles in the Order / Transformation Quadrant

Economic Principles in the Order / Transformation Quadrant

Division of Labor

Without necessarily recognizing the concept of the division of labor, humans have operated according to this universal law which was discovered by praxeology, which can be defined as action logic. The moment a choice was made for the sake of efficiency there was division of labor no matter how primitive the historical culture. It is difficult to imagine even an early stage in the history of mankind when some degree of this law did not operate. It is as old as humanity itself and it is inseparable from humans. These steps of efficiency and this production of wealth, this division of labor, is essentially the beginning of capital. Therefore it is a misconception to separate capital and labor since they are intricately interwoven, 'peas of the same pod,' and variations on the same theme.

Division of labor is expressed in the market as a type of social cooperation that comes from specialization, physical and/or intellectual specialization. The idea that the market is quietly consultative in nature, which is a very high form of cooperation, implies an intellectual division of labor or specialization, contained in the wisdom of each of the market-process participants. The increased wealth that comes from the division of labor provides incentive for such specialization. The existence of division of labor indicates that there is a desire for more goods in the economy. Division of labor brings capital into existence, provides for diverse wisdom to enter the consultative market process, generates wealth which provides incentive for even more division of labor, and it is an act of social cooperation. Mises concurs:

> In a hypothetical world in which the division of labor would not increase productivity, there would not be any society. There would not be any sentiments of benevolence and good will. [6]

Medium of Exchange

As the division of labor continued and the economy evolved it was discovered that certain goods were basic to human well-being and therefore common. Some of these basic goods were relatively less perishable and relatively easier to transport which made them valuable not only as a commodity but as a means of indirect exchange. All over the world there were a myriad of mediums of exchange that emerged from different cultures. The most universally accepted medium of exchange that emerged from the unhampered market was gold. Artificial mediums of exchange instituted by the interventionists are highly susceptible to corruption since they only exist because of a corruption of the divine economy to begin with.

Just as the market historically sifted through the alternative mediums of exchange and settled on gold, the test of a good medium of exchange is that it serves the economy and leads to further efficiencies. Confidence that it has value that cannot be destroyed, makes it an effective economic means of traversing the time element. Overcoming this time element in the economy brings with it new and wonderful possibilities.

Once a medium of exchange is in place and universally accepted then goods and services produced are valued in those terms. If there is counterfeiting of any kind then the counterfeiters, who have not contributed anything to production, cause the exchange value of the money to decrease. Subsequently, the purchasing power of the money is negatively affected, it has fallen. The counterfeiters get something for nothing but the productive members of society are ultimately stolen from. This is true no matter who is the counterfeiter, the guy down the street or the central bank.

Time Preference

Time preference is the praxeological law that explains how humans value time. All humans prefer to have whatever good or service they need now, rather than later. They prefer to have the needed good now so if they have to wait then a premium is assigned to the good. Time preference is high or low but always positive. Another way of understanding that time preference is positive is that there is always a cost involved with saving rather than consuming in the present. The higher the time preference the higher the discounting applied to the future. If people foresee war or fear for the future they will have a high time preference and will save less. In their eyes it is more costly to save. If people foresee peace and prosperity on the horizon then they have a lower time preference and will be more willing to save. A lower time preference has a reciprocal effect, it brings about a higher degree of prosperity. Let us assume that I see good things on the horizon, like peace and trustworthiness. That makes me feel secure and confident about the future. As a result I will save if I have income greater than my current needs. My savings will then, in turn, be used to advance prosperity.

Pure Rate of Interest

The premium assigned to future goods relative to the same goods in the present would represent the pure rate of interest at the individual level. The collective expression of this valuation for each culture is the pure rate of interest. The only way to get a sense of this expression of the cultural time preference is in the market since all real signals are sent in the market. The market interest rate is the pure rate of interest plus a premium to compensate for risk over time plus a factor to account for changes in the purchasing power of the money if the money is being corrupted.

To get a snapshot of the market rate of interest we look at the demand and supply of loanable funds. The amount of loanable funds available represents the supply side. The demand for loanable funds intersects the supply of loanable funds, determining the market clearing price, which approximates the pure rate of interest in an unhampered market economy. In brief, time preference is a major determinant of the supply of loanable funds and the demand for these loanable funds by entrepreneurs represents the demand side in an unhampered economy.

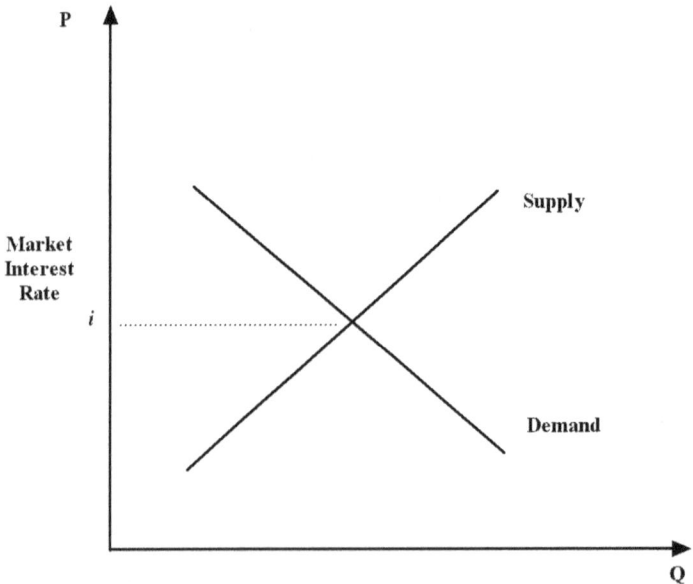

Demand and Supply of Loanable Funds

Savings

The time element of the economy causes many to become befuddled. Savings is simply the allocation of income over time. Most understand that income is allocated among various goods and services in the present. For example, I spend some of my income on housing, food, clothing and entertainment, and that is understood. Expanding on this thought, now in addition to these I also allocate a portion of my income over time as savings. Savings then translates into loanable funds. The befuddled ones miss this point.

Economic growth is limited by loanable funds. Savings is simply another way of saying loanable funds. It is true that wealthier individuals have a larger portion, in absolute and perhaps in relative terms, of their income directed into some form of savings. These are the funds that people have willingly made available for use, based on their time preferences. Now, regardless of the current stock of savings and investment the key to economic development is new and additional savings, which releases new capital for use by entrepreneurs in new productive efforts. This is what is meant by economic growth.

The market absorbs and conveys information about the present plus it conveys all of the time element information perfectly well. Essentially, the market is in divine order. It is one thing for the befuddled ones to miss the point that savings is simply an allocation of income over time, but it is quite another and more sinister thing for the befuddled ones to then impose acts of intervention on the market due to their ignorance of what savings is. An example of this would be lowering interest rates to encourage consumption and discourage savings. This act of interference is done because the interveners regard savings as the absence of consumption rather than as the conscious choice to consume at a later time. Intervention in this part of the economy, directed towards reducing savings, is extremely disruptive and destructive.

Monetary Theory

Money is a medium of exchange that permits indirect exchange and brings about all the efficiencies that result therefrom. Give consideration to these efficiencies by contrasting them with the awkwardness and impracticality of having to barter every time you wish to make an exchange.

One of the defining and determining qualities used when choosing the medium of exchange is the stock of money. Typically the medium of exchange is neither superabundant nor is it extremely rare. Once the medium of exchange is adopted in the market, because of its superior qualities and its performance as a medium of exchange, the stock of money is a non-factor. One stock of money is as good as another. If the demand for money increases it simply causes the value of each unit of money to increase. Prices of all goods and services are in terms of money so the relativities expressed in the market are maintained, which means that the market functions as always, conveying information about the relative prices of goods and services. The divine economy equilibrates quickly and it instantaneously adjusts itself to each market interaction regardless of the stock of money.

The stock of money circulates in the present and connects the present to the future through savings. Savings represents loanable funds which becomes capital. Capital then enables people to get paid now for their present services even though the 'end of the line' fruit of their work does not make it to the market until some time in the future.

In the divine economy the medium of exchange that is chosen, due to its merits, is universally accepted, partially because it cannot be manipulated artificially. In other words, no amount of alchemy can create gold out of thin air, which means that there is no such thing as a business cycle in the divine economy. God does not play games with the economy or with mankind. However, the interventionists are playing a monetary game with the economy by manipulating the stock of money. One of the most visible consequences of their intervention is the repeated occurrence of a business cycle. It is the mismanagement of the monetary system by ego-driven interventionists that causes these business cycles.

Entrepreneurship

The spirit of entrepreneurship is uniquely human. It is the quality of being alert to possibilities. It is the driving force in the economy. It has origins in the disutility of labor. Even though all human beings possess various degrees of capacity for entrepreneurship most of the time for most people it is only a potential, resting in latency. It is the interactions that take place in the market, the sparks of information there, which activates entrepreneurship. The most active entrepreneurs intentionally go to the market in an alert state methodically seeking arbitrage or other opportunities. They systematically seek prospective differences between receipts and costs in excess of the natural interest rate, taking into consideration price expectations. Some active entrepreneurs just happen to be at the right place at the right time but quickly return to latency.

There is some active entrepreneurship that is a response to a 'gut feeling' and some that comes from systematic calculation. Both are responses to opportunities, perceived from the market information. The chances of success, yielding a profit rather than a loss, are greater when the entrepreneur has systematically examined the possibilities for profit or loss before taking action.

Regardless of whether it comes about from relative novices or experienced entrepreneurs the market process is driven forward by entrepreneurship. As described by Kirzner:

> The entrepreneur's activity is essentially competitive. And this competition is inherent in the nature of the entrepreneurial market process. Or, to put it the other way around, entrepreneurship is inherent in the competitive market process. [Z]

None of this happens in a risk-free world of certainty. In fact the exact opposite is the reality. What an entrepreneur may discover to be an opportunity may never materialize. What seems like good timing may fail. Contrarily, the timing and magnitude and location of an endeavor may indeed satisfy the needs significantly more, just as alertly discerned. Profits and losses are self-regulating forces and both are inherent in the market. A market that is uncorrupted by intervention, that is, a free market, allows the entrepreneur to most clearly perceive the signals needed to serve all of our needs.

Risk

Risk is an inevitable part of the economy because there is uncertainty and imperfect knowledge. But there are market equilibrating forces that moderate risk. Savings, for one, serves to mollify risk since savings can be used to meet an immediate need or it can be directed toward production for the future. Entrepreneurs take on the role of major risk-takers and relieve others of that burden. Additionally, there is the likelihood that many of the entrepreneurs are skillful and have gained wisdom from their experiences, which skews risk towards success, lessening risk. For instance, entrepreneurs skillfully calculate economically using market information about relative prices, revenues and costs, and the availability of capital, which adds systemization and discipline to the decision-making process. If risk is of an actuarial nature then purchasing insurance will lead to a reduction of risk.

Finally, the level of charity that a society has reduces risk accordingly. If people care about one another they will give assistance when the unpredictable leads to misfortune. This lessens the risk for those affected by dire circumstances.

There is enough uncertainty and risk in the economy without more being created by the interventionists. The claim made by those who interfere with the economy is that they are reducing risk. What that actually means is that they are reducing the risk for one particular group. These ignorant or ego-driven interventionists do not and cannot fathom the negative consequences that result from their acts of interference with the market forces. Their disruption of the market process, in and of itself, increases risk for everyone, even the "protected' group. Everything becomes riskier in a hampered economy since the flow of knowledge is impeded.

Disequilibrium

The fact that there is always uncertainty and imperfect knowledge implies that the economy is constantly in flux. Errors are inherent but fleeting, are followed by fleeting inherent errors again, and so on and so on. The equilibrating forces that operate in the market, one of them being entrepreneurship, constantly purge errors. The forces underlying demand and supply move the economy towards equilibrium. Never is the economy in equilibrium but it is always tending towards it. Disequilibrium, with powerful tendencies toward equilibrium, is the norm. If errors persist and linger that indicates that the error has become institutionalized and is to some degree impermeable to market forces. All institutionalized errors are caused by human intervention and prevent the full expression of the divine potentials of the economy.

Order/Transformation Quadrant Example

Let us examine the difference between human savings and the savings of a squirrel. Apparently both anticipate the future! The squirrel's action is very strongly driven by instinct; however, if environmental conditions change significantly the squirrel will modify the size of its cache. Likewise, human savings will be modified as a consequence of conditions. Human intelligence, which can span time conceptually and which can unravel the numerous and various complexities of the world, enables man to purposefully save. Simply stated, savings is a productive and vital aspect of life.

Under the current system of intervention, its proponents come to the bizarre conclusion that savings is harmful. For example, Keynesian economics, a variant of which underlies the predominant economic systems practiced worldwide, demonizes people's choice to save. Their forced incentives to diminish savings is like force-feeding the squirrels this year only to find that their essential cache for the future is gone, ultimately leading to disaster.

Summary of the Order/Transformation Quadrant

Born from the womb of the economy are such specializations as division of labor and medium of exchange. Unborn, time seamlessly connects the present and the future economy via the price known as the pure interest rate. Savings, or the supply of loanable funds, is available to be used for economic development by entrepreneurs who see discrepancies in relative prices in the present and over extended time periods. It is interaction within the market process that transforms from latency to active each hopeful entrepreneur. Human intervention into the market distorts market signals and causes dire consequences in the present and in the future. These distortions are called malinvestments.

REAL WORLD ECONOMIC PRINCIPLES IN THE TRANSFORMATION/LAW QUADRANT

I have chosen eight economic principles for placement in this quadrant. These eight principles demonstrate reciprocal action within the continuum bounded on one side by capital and on the other by property rights. This is a fascinating quadrant since it attempts to bridge the non-transmutable nature of the law of human rights with the role of capital as it transmutes and transforms.

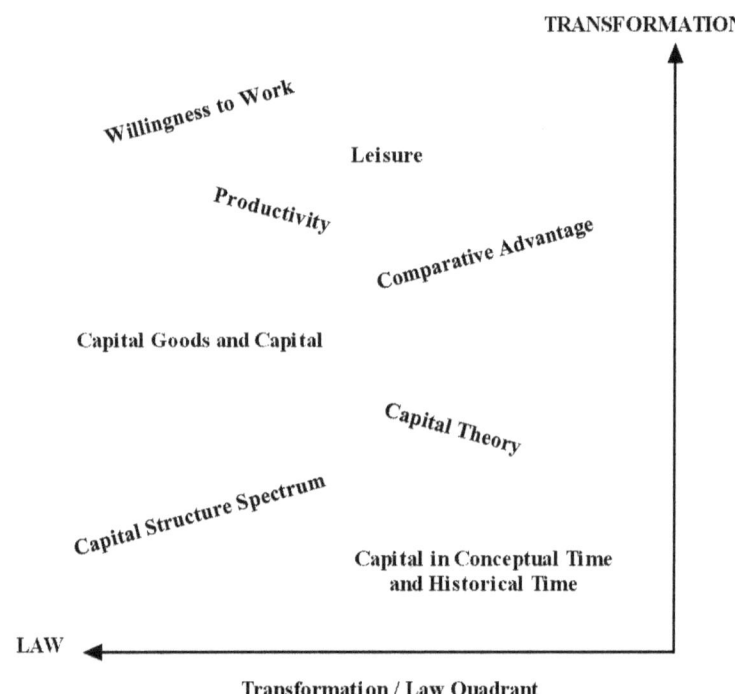

Economic Principles in the Transformation / Law Quadrant

Economic Principles in the Transformation / Law Quadrant

Willingness to Work

If we assume that there is no coercion then the first order of incentive for the human being is to meet one's own needs. Since it is possible to meet one's own needs by taking action, that is what is done. What we acquire from our labor we are able to keep. It can be deduced that this basic property right is necessary and sufficient to make a person willing to work. A negative corollary is that without the right to receive the fruits of one's labor there would be an unwillingness to work. Nothing destroys the willingness to work faster than removing the human right to 'reap what you sow.'

Leisure

Leisure is having the time to appreciate any wealth above basic subsistence. Leisure describes the circumstance that exists once all vital needs are met and a choice is then made to refrain from work to pursue something more pleasurable. Consider the significance of leisure. Not only does the transformation of labor into property give an incentive to work but acquisition of even a most rudimentary property right—here given as time to rest—gives one the right to make choices. As soon as there are choices there is the potential for leisure, for division of labor, for active entrepreneurship, and for the emergence of capital.

Productivity

This is where a new ethics of work emerges. The more productive one is the more property rights one acquires. Productivity, then, is an expression of individual initiative and it leads to increased real wages.

The more property rights one has the more choices there are, which further cascades into more loci for entrepreneurial action and more diverse types of capital investments. Technological innovation springs from these diverse types of capital investments. Guess what? All of these lead to increased productivity. Operating within this milieu is the productive actions of businessmen and the users of capital and it is their actions that generate profits. A portion of these profits then goes towards new capital in the form of wages and factor incomes. Businessmen and women and the users of capital play a guiding role, as stated by Mises:

> What produces the product are not toil and trouble in themselves, but the fact that the toiling is guided by reason. The human mind alone has the power to remove uneasiness. [8]

This advancing productivity is thoroughly described by Reisman:

> The precise nature of the work of businessmen and capitalists needs to be explained. In essence, it is to raise the productivity, and thus the real wages, of manual labor by means of creating, coordinating, and improving the efficiency of the division of labor. [9]

The cascading continues—if I am more productive, then my real wage will increase, which will translate into more savings provided the future is perceived as hopeful. This will create new capital which will increase productivity. Productivity can be defined as more consumer goods per productive unit. As the supply of goods increases the price of those goods decreases, which means an increase in the standard of living in real terms. What can be discerned from this is that property rights, which underlie productivity, serve as the foundation for development.

Comparative Advantage

Nowhere is economics more remarkable than in the law of comparative advantage. Comparative advantage is another derivation of relativity. Regardless of absolute advantage every person or demographic unit has a comparative advantage relative to their trading partners. Implied in trade (exchange) is the double inequality in exchange. Trade only happens if both sides benefit.

The resources that are uniquely mine as part of my skills and my property rights are such that I have a comparative advantage with regards something, relative to my trading partners' skills and property rights. If we engage in trade, the fact that we do trade means that we both have gained. The gain is in some degree an advancement which then can be consumed or otherwise used to expand my property rights, possibly into capital goods, either directly or indirectly through savings.

Comparative advantage is a combination of the principle of division of labor and the principle of relativity. Regardless of absolute ability there is always a productive advantage in relative terms. Therefore, so that I can take full advantage of the trading opportunity, I will specialize in producing the good or service in which I have the relative advantage.

Capital Goods and Capital

These are intermediate goods or producer goods which make it possible for consumer goods and services to be made more readily available and/or of higher quality. Capital goods initially require the use of capital to pay the wages of those making or using the capital goods until there is a flow of income from the 'end of the line' consumer good or service. It is easy to see that capital exists in different stages of development. Some capital goods are already completed and are producing goods. Other capital is tied up in capital goods which still are not completed and still are not producing goods.

Capital is a loan of the fruits of past labor. The users of capital, capitalists, pay for the factors needed, either as wages or as incomes to the other factors (both of which are costs to the capitalist). If the returns to capital are greater than the costs of capital then the capital value increases. If new or free capital becomes available it is alertly used since it is the most limiting factor in the economy. Just as economic growth is limited by capital, which originates from loanable funds (savings), consumption is limited by production.

There is such a severe prejudice towards the word 'capitalist.' The historical reason for this prejudice is outside the realm of this book. In the divine economy the capitalist is a real and vital agent of the economy just like time is a vital element, or entrepreneurs are vital agents, or property rights is a vital element. This book makes it clear repeatedly that there is a great deal of ignorance about economics and so there are many prejudices to be overcome. Mises broadens the view toward productive capital:

> Production is not something physical, material, and external; it is a spiritual and intellectual phenomenon. Its essential requisites are not human labor and external natural forces and things, but the decision of the mind to use these factors as means for the attainment of ends. [10]

The education that is necessary for remedying the problems of economic prejudice and ignorance will not come from institutions that are funded by the interventionists. This book is one of the ways to gain clarity about economics, independent of contemporary prejudices.

Capital Theory

Of all the factors in the economy capital is the most limiting. Why? Look back at the sections about loanable funds and time preference. People strongly prefer things in the present. Therefore even under the most peaceful conditions only a small proportion of their incomes will be saved. Whereas the other half of the loanable funds market is the demand for loanable funds and that is a function of the determined search for capital in the market.

Capital is the most limiting factor in the economy because it is constrained by loanable funds. The economy is also most limited by capital since capital is the transformational element of the economy which, of course, would make it highly sought after. Remember the earlier discussion of the efficiency gain from division of labor, well; it is capital that yields a cumulative and collective efficiency gain for the economy that dwarfs all of the other economic factors. Capital is the key to progress.

Once the primitive economy moved beyond individuals being self-sufficient but barely subsistent, capital became the means of payment to labor and other factors used in the production of goods. In reality there is no rivalry between labor and capital except in the fictional model of the world imagined by Marx and those who are like-minded, where capital is selectively excluded from the economy. Labor is intimately and ultimately the beneficiary of capital as are the owners of the other factors of production.

Let us consider the economically relevant subject of the formation of capital. Here, disutility of labor is a motivating element, as is time preference (which determines the level of savings). Refer to the interactive three-way relationship in Diagram F. Division of labor, a specialization that is an expression of human diversity, creates in the market loci for arbitrage and profit opportunities. This quickly draws the attention of alert entrepreneurs. Savings are then used as capital to pay wages and factor incomes until the time when revenues can. Sales revenue minus the money costs (wages and factor incomes) eventually yields a profit (or a loss). Some of the net income then re-enters as loanable funds, as 'new' capital.

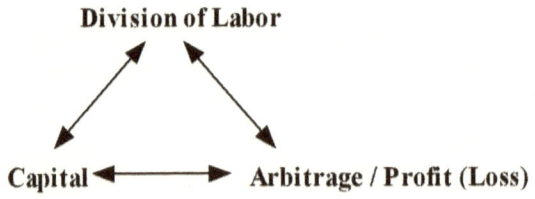

Division of Labor

Capital ⟷ **Arbitrage / Profit (Loss)**

Diagram F—Interactive Three-way Relationship

Another interesting economic benefit from capital is the actual generation of information about both revenues and costs as a result of the application of capital in the economy. It is the involvement in the economy by capitalists that creates wages and factor prices (these are their costs) and sales revenues. These wage and factor prices serve as a source of information, enabling entrepreneurs and capitalists to calculate so they can make rational decisions. If we assume these decisions are from the market signals in a divine economy, they are fully compatible with the divine concepts of unity and justice.

In a 'Crusoe' situation, one person isolated on an island, the initial payment for his initial work (his wage) equals his profit. He works by climbing a coconut tree and he eats the coconut (profit). At that point the wage to profit ratio is equal to one. Once there is an opportunity to specialize (trading with others in a market) and there is savings, capital enters into the scenario, which generates wages and factor incomes. To see how capital benefits labor, see Diagram G. If there are profits then that will end up creating 'new' savings. Also, above average rates of return will attract more capitalists. As the number of capitalists increases wages and factor incomes increase because there is competition for these scarce resources which put upward pressure on the wages and factor prices. Division of labor at the early stages near 'Crusoe' was crude but as it is directed by business-men and capitalists, division of labor becomes more refined. The process contin-ues. Generation of wealth not only brings more capitalists to the market but it also leads to an expansion of the use of capital to more temporally remote pro-duction processes. As the number of capitalists increases, the profits tend to decrease with each getting a smaller portion, independent of the wages and factor incomes paid out during production. In other words, wages and factor incomes tend to increase while profits tend to decrease. Additionally, every innovation and improvement that comes from this process ultimately reaches the consumers who benefit from both better products and lower prices brought about by innovation. In summary, the wage to profit ratio increases as civilization advances. There is a tendency toward a uniform rate of return on all capital invested which closely approximates the pure rate of interest. Mises makes a similar observation:

> The history of mankind is the record of a progressive intensification of the division of labor—The operation of the principle of division of labor and its corollary, cooperation, tends ultimately toward a world-embracing system of production. [11]

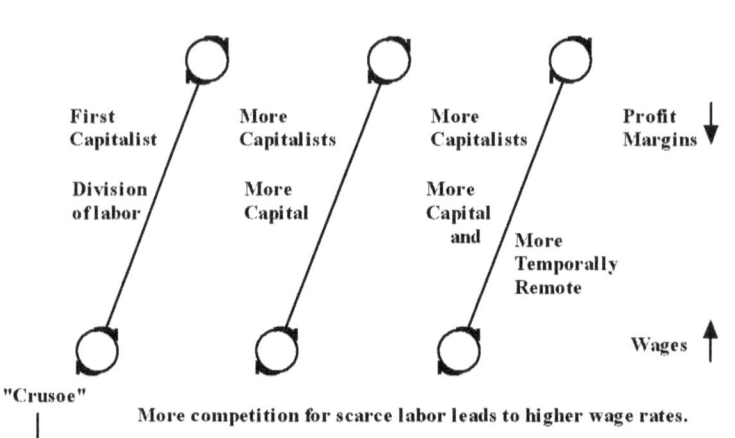

Ever-Advancing Economy

Diagram G–Capital Benefits Labor

Business cycles do not occur in the divine economy since none of the signals in the market are distorted. The market interest rate truly reflects the amount of savings that people have, creating a balance throughout the capital structure between the present and the future. When an artificial interest rate is created by the deceitful practices associated with fiat currencies the entrepreneurs allocate capital incorrectly, in both the amount invested and the capital invested temporally across the time horizon, which leads to a business cycle.

If we make an assumption that there is only one act of intervention, then all the malinvestments would be purged by the divine economy during the passage of one business cycle. But since resources are allocated across a span of time and across a spectrum of capital structure, a business cycle is not merely something that happens at one specific point in time. The negative consequences manifest themselves over many time periods until all the malinvestments are purged for the duration of that cycle.

If consumer credit is extended in the market artificially, which means that it is unmatched by existing savings, capital is consumed. What is happening is that consumption is in excess of the productive capacity. Productive capacity in the economy is determined by the level of savings and the subsequent capital. The only way to consume more now is to use current savings, which were to serve as the loanable funds for 'new' capital and economic growth. This is the equivalent of consuming capital which will then cause the economy to regress, the typical consequence of intervention.

The important point to note here is that the divine economy heals itself and cannot be destroyed. All disruption and disorder in the economy comes from corruption caused by human intervention. Equilibrating forces clear these afflictions almost immediately after they are halted. Rest assured that the power of the divine economy is indestructable and self-healing.

Capital Structure Spectrum

Production of all types requires capital. Some capital may be needed for a short time like a week or a month. Other capital suffices production for years. The picture that emerges is a wide array of production, funded for varying lengths of time, all of which makes up the capital structure funded by savings.

The starting point of an endeavor is significant. If there is capital available at the beginning then the scale of production can be of a greater magnitude. Likewise, the temporal remoteness from the consumer good can be greater, in other words there can be more research and development, which ultimately makes the possible fruits of the endeavor greater.

The concept of originary interest [12] is closely related to time preference but it can be used to explain a different aspect of the economy. Originary interest is another of the praxeological laws that describes how humans act. People act in a way such that they value present goods higher than those same goods in the future, in relative terms. In and of itself originary interest explains why people take action in the present. Without this conceptual reality operating in the human psyche there would be no consumption since there would be no preference for anything now. Humans devoid of originary interest would have no motivation to eat now, in the present, which would cause the species to go extinct. Needless to say, human beings do, indeed, place a high valuation on the present.

Considering the points just made it becomes clear is that capital structure is really a spectrum. The most immediate end of the spectrum is consumption. The more roundabout means of production, those that are temporally remote from the consumer, are located towards the other end of the spectrum. The capital structure spectrum is a conceptual representation of the various forms of capital over time. This idea of one spectrum for all the various forms or structures of capital serves as another proof of the inseparability of capital from the choices made to sustain and satisfy life. There is nothing evil about capital, in fact, capital is simply vital, as vital as your life vein!

Capital in Conceptual Time and Historical Time

When there appears to be no time other than the present (t=0) the originary interest tells us that all consumption would be immediate. There would be no savings. When the time horizon expands (t +1) originary interest tells us that priority is given to the present time but a pool of funding will begin to form unless the economy is in a condition of basic subsistence. Conceptual time shows that capital inevitably forms.

When the economy began in its simplest form at t=0 the effort made just for survival meant that the gain (profit) was equivalent to the compensation for the labor (wage). As the economy evolved (t + 1) and progressed past subsistence, due to the development of division of labor, capital became available to pay wages and factor incomes (money costs). 'Revenues minus costs' information brings about the ability to calculate which then enables the entrepreneurs to drive the economy forward. Historical time shows that capital serves to continually increase the ratio of wage/profit (wage>profit). Labor and factors are the beneficiaries of capital.

Transformation/Law Quadrant Example

Comparative advantage operates in human society because human beings are complex and they have a plethora of needs and wants. To some extent geographic distances act as a limitation. Since there are numerous trading partners with a great diversity of special skills and talents, all of whom also have a great number of needs, the law of comparative advantage operates without fail.

This law can be violated causing great harm to all and especially to those whose alternatives are most limited. One example of intervention that does this type of damage is any kind of trade barrier, for example, tariffs. A simple regional economy may need to have free access to markets for their comparative advantage to be realized. Tariffs may destroy the feasibility of its comparative advantage, depriving this simple regional economy of the ability to transform itself. Without such interference the law of comparative advantage would activate all the agents of prosperity: division of labor, savings, capital, and entrepreneurship—assuming property rights exist.

Summary of the Transformation/Law Quadrant

The divine economy rests firmly on property rights. In contrast, what suffers most in an economy hampered by weak property rights is people's willingness to save and the ability for capital to accumulate. The economy then loses its power to transform. The divine economy has an intricate capital structure which acts as an agent of transformation leading to economic development. Built into the divine economy are all the incentives that encourage movement towards choice and the use of capital.

REAL WORLD ECONOMIC PRINCIPLES IN THE LAW/HUMAN SPIRIT QUADRANT

I have chosen five economic principles for placement in this quadrant. What we have here is the blending of the human spirit, as it operates according to the universal laws inherent in the human operating system; blended with a legal framework that is based on the divine principle of justice. At the heart of the divine economy is the transcendental property right—transcendental because there is no real separation between property rights and human rights. As presented by Rothbard:

> In the first place, there are senses in which property rights are identical with human rights: one, that property can only accrue to humans, so that their rights to property are rights that belong to human beings; and two, that the person's right to his own body, his personal liberty, is a property right in his own person as well as a 'human right.'[13]

All the various forms of human rights are merely different types of property rights and serve as a protection of the human spirit. Enforcement of law is within its proper bounds when limited to defense of the rights of personal property and against violent intervention.

Private ownership of the means of production benefits everyone since the fruits of those means of production go to everyone via the market. This is part of a continuous and progressive process and it translates into a rising standard of living. Prosperity, which can be defined as an ever-improving standard of living for everyone, is the outcome of exercising property rights in an unhampered market.

Economic Principles in the Law / Human Spirit Quadrant

Economic Principles in the Law / Human Spirit Quadrant

Subjective Valuation

Each person is unique and has unique interests—that is, both in the array of interests and the degree of interests. Each choice made is a reflection of that person's subjective valuation. Subjective valuations do not have an empirical nature to them. There is no number that represents your like or dislike of an orange. Nor is there a need for such a representation since the market perfectly handles each subjective choice instantaneously and in combination with all the other relative choices. Subjective valuation is a human right emanating from the human spirit.

Consumer Sovereignty

Human beings are created noble, created in the image of God. The world and all of its wonders are for the glory and exaltation of humanity. In the end, all things in this world serve mankind. When a desire is manifested as a choice there is an opportunity for some of the resources of the world to be directed towards meeting that desire. In a sense all forces are mobilized to answer the command of the king—the consumer. The entrepreneur, by nature, is alert to these opportunities and perceives the signals sent in the market. The motion set in order by the entrepreneur moves resources towards whatever means are needed to satisfy the consumer—the king. Production of goods and services to satisfy the king—the consumer—necessitates that the producers hire labor and other resources. In that way all of the 'subjects' benefit from their service to the 'king.' Wherever in the economy the consumers spend more the profits rise, which stimulates economic competition, followed by investment and production. In other words, the pattern of investment and production follows the consumer spending pattern, in obedience to the 'king.'

What if a righteous person notices that the consumers are choosing foolish things? Although the divine economy is always in operation, the degree of the maturity of humanity is always in a state of imperfection. The present location of the ever-advancing economy along the spiritual maturity spectrum is due to the state of perfection that mankind has reached and due to the amount of hindrance in the divine economy by intervention. Relative to the future, humanity at the present is immature, but relative to the past humanity is advancing toward higher ideals and values.

Ever-Advancing Economy

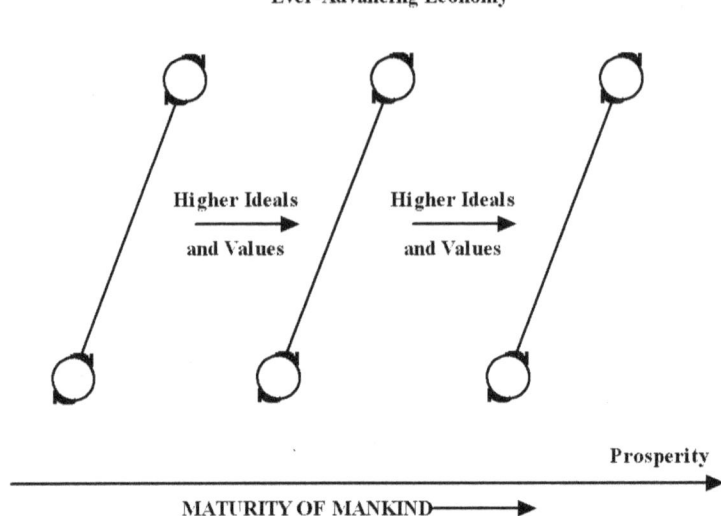

The divine economy is not to be blamed for the present shortcomings evident in humankind. Instead, intervention needs to be removed so that information can flow freely and so that the divine virtues inherent in human beings can be 'acquired' and 'polished.'

Purchasing Power of Money

Money is the medium of exchange that enables the benefits of indirect exchange to permeate the market. It has value relative to all the other goods in the economy. The value of the money in my possession is my property, in other words, it is a property right of mine. If I can expect to get 2 pounds of sugar for one dollar but instead, surreptitiously, I receive only one pound it is clear that there has been a theft. Fifty cents was quietly taken from me.

Likewise, if the money is debased by deliberate actions, everyone who uses the money is a victim. Stealing from everyone equally does not make such an act a just act by any righteous definition.

The value of money finds its real definition in the market relative to other goods and services but it is based on the demand for money and the supply of money. If there is the ability to print money without respecting property rights (counterfeiting and central bank inflation, as examples) then the purchasing power of money, its value, will decline. All holders of money will then have their property rights violated.

Contracts

The purpose of contracts is to provide a legal framework for protecting private property and market operations. The gains from trade and exchange can be extended by ensuring payments and by ensuring delivery under contract. Protecting private property encourages savings and the accretion of capital across the time horizon which raises the standard of living for everyone.

Ownership: There can be only one person, or any of the larger entities of ownership, that has the exclusive rights to a particular piece of property at the same time.

Rent and Interest: Ownership of land or of a durable good or of loanable funds confers the right to portion it out to others and to charge them for its use. Ownership does not necessarily equate with use. Use does not define ownership.

Insurance: The providers of this type of contract define the risk groups and discriminate between risk groups and establish a contractual relationship with the client based on actuarial data.

Standard of Living

A standard of living needs to be measured in real terms, not in nominal terms. In real terms the standard of living increases as capital increases and as division of labor takes place. To see how capital, incrementally new capital, leads to an improved standard of living refer to Diagram H. In other words, as productivity increases real wages increase even while market competition is pushing the economy towards a uniform rate of return on capital.

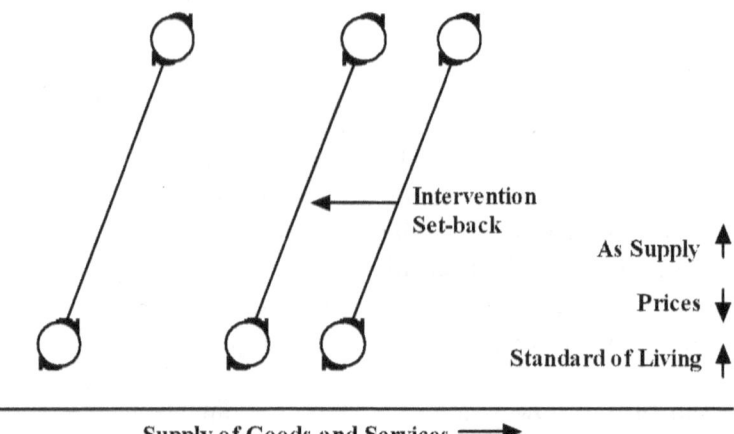

Diagram H–Capital Advances Standard of Living

Increases in nominal wage rates without increases in productivity are attributed to inflation of the money supply and can be traced back to the interventionists. Under these conditions the standard of living is decreasing in real terms despite nominal increases.

Here is the vision of the standard of living that is possible in an unhampered economy, the divine economy. As capital increases, productivity increases which causes the supplies of goods and services to increase, causing their prices to decrease. Since productivity is increasing, in turn, real wages are increasing, which means that the standard of living is increasing. As the standard of living increases the perception of hope and prosperity increases which means that the time preference lowers. A lower time preference translates into more savings which brings us back to the beginning of this cycle, an increase in capital, resulting from an increase in savings. Notice the trends—prices decrease, real income increases, the standard of living increases and prosperity increases.

Law/Human Spirit Quadrant Example

The divine economy rests on the foundation that each and every human being is created in the image of God and that each one is unique. Unique in the sense that there are no two alike, never were and never will be. How could there be anything other than subjective valuation in the human realm, then, by definition? If we are all different in the array of qualities of spirit and fabric then we will always intellectually function subjectively.

This is not a problem scientifically, as long as the proper methodology is used. Applying the objective methodology of the natural sciences, as if we operate like atoms within a molecule, is inappropriate. Many of the economic fallacies, today propagated as economic facts, were derived from trying to use objective methodology upon a creature which is subjective by nature.

Only the subjective methodology can accommodate free will. Free will is another foundation piece of the divine economy since all of the actors in the economy have free will. Free will is also a foundation of the creation of humankind; it is part of human nature. It manifests itself in the independence of each decision made within the mind of each person—which is subjective valuation. Each decision is unique to the circumstances deemed important by each individual, who are themselves unique.

Summary of the Law/Human Spirit Quadrant

The really important part of this quadrant of the model is that there is a link to law; laws that provide a legal framework to support property rights, and laws of human action. The legal framework that supports property rights recognizes the importance of contracts and regards wholesale theft, such as the inflation of the money supply, as a crime, just as it does any other violation of contract.

From a legal point of view there is a way to protect the economy from fraudulent practices. Individuals or individuals collectively can seek clarity and justice by refining the definitions of property rights and then by insisting that they are protected.

Inherently and in accordance with the laws of human action, the divine economy allows diverse expression, it satisfies human needs, and it leads to an ever-advancing prosperity.

4

Policy

How do we get from the history of economic thought to useful steps for improving the economy? How can a model which is built upon recognition of the spiritual nature of man be of value in the real world? What good is it to tie economic principles to the modus operandi of the divine economy if there are no practical fruits? This is where policy comes in. It is a bridge between the theory and the application.

There are two things that I tried to clearly present about the divine economy. One is that it is powerful and transcendent, yet ever-present and nurturing. The other point of clarity is that the divine economy can be put into a corrupted or diseased condition by human intervention. The divine economy can never be destroyed, as evidenced by its equilibrating forces, but knowledge can be stifled and signals distorted by ego-driven intervention into the market process.

Knowing that the full potential of the divine economy can only be reached when intervention ceases may lead one to think that there should be no intervening policy. Contrarily, knowing that the justice that is inherent in the divine economy can only be reached if the market is free may lead one to think that there are policy steps to take to protect the divine economy from intervention, for the benefit of all mankind.

Well Defined and Continually Refined Property Rights

It is clear that everything rests on property rights, which are mirror images of human rights. Not a single thing can happen that honors a person's human rights without acknowledging that these are his property rights. Once this most basic right, the human right/property right, is defined the market process begins. As the property rights are refined the divine economy will empower human civilization to advance. Without secure private property there will be little savings and investment and therefore little prosperity.

What is the seed of property/human rights? The first clue comes from Immanuel Kant:

> "Freedom…is the only original right belonging to every man by virtue of his humanity."[14]

Policy Statement: A rational and just policy would be to develop law—laws that specifically define, refine and protect property rights in terms such that they are treated and considered as basic human rights.

The Right of Secession

At the social level the corollary of freedom implied in individual property rights is the right of secession. For a jurisdiction to guarantee its prosperity it will have to be able to secure property rights which may mean removing itself from the yoke of the oppressor.

Policy Statement: A rational policy would be to develop law in such a way that a jurisdiction would not have to accept any intervention that a larger jurisdiction tried to impose upon its economy.

Market Forces Will Moderate Business Sizes

In a market free from intervention firms can naturally become only so large. The inefficiencies of bureaucracy limit its size. For example, if a firm is vertically integrated—originally expanded in this manner to capture efficiency—but it becomes excessively large, then it begins to lose the ability to rationally allocate resources. Wages and factor prices in the internal (in-house) market begin to have no connection to the real market, become distorted and unrealistic, preventing the firm from being able to calculate. Smaller firms without these errors will begin to out-compete these overly bureaucratic firms. When interventionist laws protect certain types of business ownerships by limiting the liability of the owners, it artificially encourages these firms to become very large since they are protected from the costs associated with damages to property rights of independent third parties. Therefore, limited liability for corporations causes distortions. Protection of property rights will ultimately make the economy serve the whole of mankind with justice rather than favoring institutions that are narrowly created by vested interests.

Policy Statement: A rational and just policy would be to remove the barriers that prevent property rights from being protected and remove the special privileges that artificially protect any entity from the equilibrating forces of the divine economy.

Enforcement of Property Rights

The main policy recommendation derived from the divine economy model is to continually refine the definition of property rights. The corollary to this is to strengthen the legal system such that it can enforce property rights. Both the definition of property rights and the ability to enforce property rights are currently weak, even weaker than they were 100 years ago. Needless to say the direction of that trend is wrongly oriented, away from progress, and needs to be set aright.

Policy Statement: A rational policy would be to initially begin enforcing property rights at the level of the individual, and then to learn how best to refine property rights from these efforts. Each community has this right and responsibility. The role of government is simply to protect its citizens from fraud or acts of violence by enforcing property rights.

Education About Entrepreneurship

Another policy that surfaces from looking at the divine economy model is: to educate people about latent and active entrepreneurship. The purpose of educating people about entrepreneurship is basically to encourage the acquisition of the skill of discernment. This comes from learning about the learning process. The more discernment and alertness there is in the market the more quickly knowledge will flow and the more quickly will it be acted upon. This leads to an advancement of the market process and to prosperity. If the market is in an inefficient condition the solution is to educate people about entrepreneurship not to corrupt the divine economy by intervention.

Policy Statement: A rational policy would be to encourage all providers of education to acknowledge the role of entrepreneurship in advancing prosperity and to teach skills that help to make people discerning and alert.

War and Inflation Violate Property Rights

Another policy that emerges from the divine economy model places emphasis again on education. It is clear from the concepts in the divine economy model that if people can trust the future they will have lower time preferences which will amplify the transforming capability of capital. There are very specific interventions into the economy that strongly influence the level of trust. If there is a tendency to choose war as the main or even as a viable alternative then the lessened trust that such an act engenders atrophies the economy. Or if there is a medium of exchange that can easily be debased by a central bank then the horizon of the time preference shortens, stifling prosperity. Both of these acts of intervention, war and inflation by the central bank, violate the property rights of humanity. Those things that foster trust and trustworthiness need to be given particular emphasis as part of the learning process.

Policy Statement: War and its exorbitant costs and its destruction, and inflation of the money supply by the central bank, are unacceptable violations of property rights and those who try to impose either of these should be held accountable by legal means. Authority to take these actions needs to be specifically assigned so that there is specific and definite accountability. Legal liability for such acts needs to be given precedence over the veil of government self-protection.

Gold Passes the Market Test

Inflation reduces the purchasing power of money; and it causes the redistribution of wealth towards the favored ones of the interventionists. Both of these represent theft of private property and both are acts of injustice. The free market chose gold as the medium of exchange because it optimizes the characteristics determined by the market to be necessary for a trustworthy medium of exchange. Strongly preventing dishonest and untrustworthy acts by the interventionists is certainly a good reason to return to the gold standard.

Free banking, where banks compete against each other for the trust of their customers, is almost completely sufficient to safeguard against fraudulent banking practices. Combined with refined and enforced property rights it is wholly sufficient. Free banking is a very important component of a divine economy since it has the merits of self-regulation and since it serves the people, instead of masking insolvency as is the case with current banking practices. Having a strong and honest banking system will encourage savings.

Policy Statement: Clear the banking system of all of its barriers and restrictions—these are acts of intervention designed to control the economy and to direct wealth towards the ego-driven interventionists—and let the market determine if the current system is a viable one. Legal tender laws are unnecessary in a divine economy where the medium of exchange is universally recognized because of its independence and its other merits.

Counteract the Misinformation About Capital

There is a very difficult educational task ahead to counteract the institutionalized prejudice against capitalism. Capital has been maligned and misunderstood for so long that most people feel that capital is not a part of themselves, that it is outside of themselves. One goal of the educator will be to help people to see that every choice or act to improve oneself is capital-made-manifest. And the improvement made is then an advancement and the starting point for the next step. Appreciation of capital, when seen as honoring one's own progress, will go a long way towards reversing the poisonous bigotry directed at capital, which permeates the world today. The anti-capitalist mentality is a poison emanating from Marxism, socialism and much of empirical economics. It is a combination of their atheism and their adherence to an incorrect methodology for the social sciences that leads them to remove capital from its place in the human psyche. The force that declares capital to be a vital part of the human operating system—the divine economy itself—shuns their ill-fated attempt.

Policy Statement: Encourage providers of education to recognize that every improvement an individual makes, their education for example, is a form of capital. Then, instead of spreading negative impressions about capital, the education system will compliment itself for being a contributor to capital around the world and will empower the next generation with knowledge about this factor—capital—which is significant since it is the most limiting factor in the economy.

New Capital is a Good Start

Assuming that some of those who use this book will be concerned about an economy that is undeveloped (although this same principle operates in a more advanced economy) the first steps taken should be to encourage and nurture capital. Unprotected property rights is very often the reason people do not save. Any steps that secure property and foster trustworthiness lead to the emergence of new capital. New capital advances productivity and then the development process begins.

Policy Statement: Recognize that having secure property rights leads to savings and new capital which begins the advancement towards prosperity.

International Free Trade

Another self-evident policy recommendation is to recognize that the divine economy works at all times and regardless of scale. The same benefits that come to an individual when taking part in exchange in the market occur at the international level with trade. Only international free trade allows the prosperity of the divine economy to be fully released. Artificial and imaginary boundary restrictions are simply interventions that lessen the prosperity that can come from the divine economy. Only international division of labor under a system of secure property rights and free trade brings the resources of the world to the market efficiently and with justice, for all to enjoy.

Policy Statement: All trade barriers interfere with the divine economy and cause unnecessary suffering. Free trade agreements are acts of intervention and are a misnomer. Free trade is, in reality, action not words and it will happen automatically if the ego-driven interventionists are removed from the picture.

The Moral Authority of the Divine Economy

To quote Ludwig von Mises: 'The first condition for the establishment of perpetual peace is the general adoption of the principles of laissez-faire capitalism.'[15] I would like to modify his recommendation slightly. First, rest assured that the prosperity of an ever-advancing civilization emanates from the divine economy. Second, trust in the equilibrating power of the divine economy. Third, trust in the divine justice that comes from protecting property rights and that comes from recognizing that property rights are human rights.

Those who fail to admit their own limitations and expect others to believe their assertions that they can comprehend all that is going on in the economy—thereby giving them the right to interfere—these are the ones who are now without authority. It matters not what position one holds or what degree one has or what record of publication one has. There is no human act of intervention in the economy that is not feeble-minded when compared with the omnipotent and omnipresent nature of God. All interference with the economy is necessarily ego-driven; and it lacks moral authority. The economy is a divine institution in the domain of human action and all human action emanates from the human operating system, which is divine—created in the image of God.

Epilogue

The divine economy model introduced in Chapter Two is a gem. It is a powerful tool for bringing economic principles into the light for further examination. From this point forward I propose to you that the science of economics, which is often referred to as the 'dismal science,' is instead seen as a bright and hopeful study of purposeful human action!

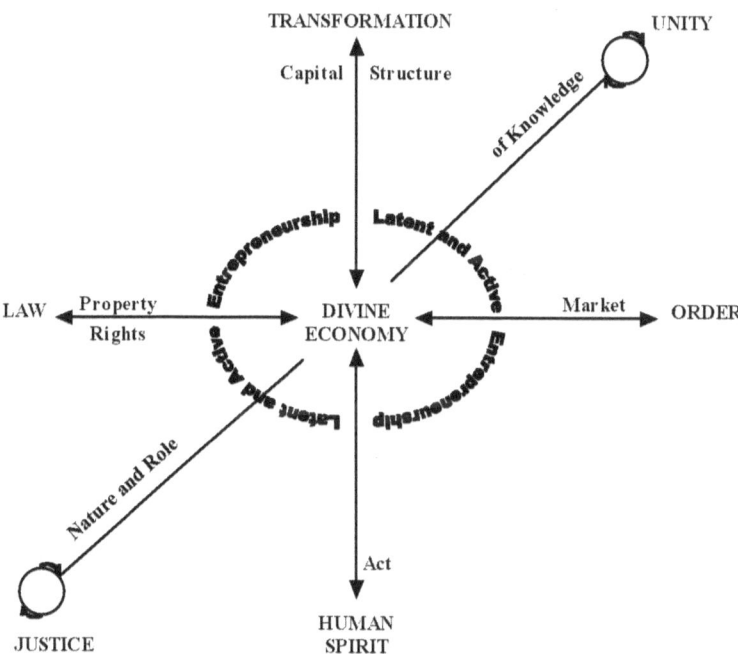

I have written this book to uncover what seemed to be hidden and to connect it to the vast economic knowledge that emerged from classical liberalism. My goal with this book is to make clear much of the mystery about how the economy works and to make it clear that there is no justification for human interference.

I have played a useful role by creating, in this work, a palatable and moral economics model as suggested by Ludwig von Mises:

> The flowering of human society depends on two factors: the intellectual power of outstanding men to conceive sound social and economic theories, and the ability of these or other men to make these ideologies palatable to the majority. [16]

List of References

[1] Ludwig von Mises, *Human Action*, Fourth Revised Edition (San Francisco: Fox & Wilkes, 1996), p. 3.

[2] Ibid., p. 882.

[3] F. A. Hayek, *The Use of Knowledge in Society*, The American Economic Review, Volume XXXV, Number Four, September 1945: p. 528.

[4] Murray N. Rothbard, *Man Economy and State*, second edition, Scholar's Edition (Ludwig von Mises Institute, 2004), p. 1124.

[5] Bartolome de Albornoz, *Arte de los Contratos* (Valencia, 1573), Ch. 7, 29.

[6] Ludwig von Mises, *Human Action*, Fourth Revised Edition (San Francisco: Fox & Wilkes, 1996), p. 145.

[7] Israel M. Kirzner, *Competition & Entrepreneurship* (Chicago, University of Chicago Press, 1973), pp. 16-17.

[8] Ludwig von Mises, *Human Action*, Fourth Revised Edition (San Francisco: Fox & Wilkes, 1996), p. 142.

[9] George Reisman, *Classical Economics vs. The Exploitation Theory*, The Political Economy of Freedom Essays in Honor of F. A. Hayek, Edited by Kurt R. Leube and Albert H. Zlabinger (München and Wien: Philosophia Verlag, The International Carl Menger Library, 1985).

[10] Ludwig von Mises, *Human Action*, Fourth Revised Edition (San Francisco: Fox & Wilkes, 1996), p. 142.

[11] Ibid., *Theory and History* (The Ludwig von Mises Institute, 1985), p. 234-5.

[12] Ibid., *Human Action*, Fourth Revised Edition (San Francisco: Fox & Wilkes, 1996), p. 526.

[13] Murray N. Rothbard, *The Ethics of Liberty* (New York: New York University Press, 1998), p. 113.

[14] Immanuel Kant, *The Metaphysics of Morals*, tr. and ed. Mary Gregor, with an intro. by Roger Sullivan (Cambridge University Press, 1996).

[15] Ludwig von Mises, *The Ultimate Foundation of Economic Science* (Kansas City: Scheed Andrews & Mcmeel, 1978), p. 137.

[16] Ibid., *Human Action*, Fourth Revised Edition (San Francisco: Fox & Wilkes, 1996), p. 985.

978-0-595-35083-4
0-595-35083-6

www.ingramcontent.com/pod-product-compliance
Lightning Source LLC
Chambersburg PA
CBHW021018180526
45163CB00005B/2009